Deception, Distraction, and Duck Calls

How to share your Faith with just a Duck Call

Written By
Benjamin "Bear" Lyle

Custom Callmaker & Owner of BearKraft Game Calls

ISBN:151484611X
ISBN-13: 9781514846117

CONTENTS

FOREWORD

WARNING: This book is not politically correct, grammatically perfect, or professionally written.

It's been written specifically for Waterfowlers, but the concepts within go much deeper and can be beneficial for anyone that desires to share the Christian Faith on a simpler yet meaningful platform.

As you read through the book, I hope that you'll take the time to reflect on your own everyday life and how you may be able to use something simple to express the Love of Christ to those around you in creative and interesting ways.

1 INTRO

Not much different than an elusive member of the waterfowl family, we are all pursued by a force greater than we'd like to give credence to. Regardless of our awareness, vigilance, or unwavering dedication to not be overtaken, it has a way of creeping into our lives and rocking the boat of what we consider to be "normal". I use the term "normal", because I think that's what we all strive for, but none of us really use it for what it means. "Normal" means average, expected, typical and fundamentally boring! So, when did "normal" become a good thing? We like to use it in the context of; holding to a standard for everyday life that we would refer to as "A-Okay" or "Life is Good". Simple enough, "normal" became a good thing when everything else got BAD!!

When that spread of decoys you were flying into for breakfast became a melodramatic version of Nintendo's "DuckHunt", or when you heard the shotgun blasts ring out from a timber hole as you were frantically looking for a place to rest, it's not much different for animals than it is for humans. When things get bad, we all have similar emotions. Fear and panic usually come first followed by sadness or sometimes anger depending on the situation. Finally, once the shock wears off and you get a basic comprehension of what's going on, we're filled with an overwhelming desire for things to return to "normal". When things are going great and you're on top of the world, you don't say things like, "Whew, I'll be glad when things get back to normal around here!" "Normal" is taken for granted far too often.

To get back to the original point, something is constantly stalking us, hunting us, and strategically using whatever tactics available to make us fall into temptation and ultimately draw us away from God's hand of protection. Regardless of what you may call it; Evil, Satan, the Devil, or the man downstairs, his tactics are plentiful and effective, but nevertheless teeming with lies.

> ....for he is a liar and the father of lies.
> John 8:44

Evil is sometimes allowed to disrupt our "normal", but how we react to that disruption is what determines its effect on our lives.

2 DECEPTION

Camouflage, decoys, and duck calls are all essentially harmless objects, but when used together with a specific purpose, they become powerful tools of deception. These tools are time tested and field proven to coordinate a harvest of thousands of ducks across the continent every year.

Camouflage is one of the most important of these tools and is the go-to garb of hunters everywhere. Camouflage has a purpose: to disguise or hide the presence of something by making it blend in with its surroundings. We all understand the benefit of camo while hunting, but can we identify when its being used against us? Rarely is it obvious, nor perceivable in our own situation, but many things in everyday life are merely camouflaged tripwires waiting to send us tumbling head first into a pit of darkness. More about camouflage later.

Decoys have a specific purpose too. They are used by hunters to create a feeling of comfort and safety so that ducks believe there are others that have already committed to a given area. Some ducks, despite their better judgment, can be sold on these features alone, but others need a bit more convincing. The hunter's use of camouflage prevents the primary threat from being identified while the decoys give the illusion that everyone else is doing it! Ever heard of "peer pressure"? How often we ignore the consequences or fail to see what may be lurking nearby as a result of feeling there is "safety in numbers". The use of a decoy undoubtedly preys on that feeling and is THE oldest trick in the book! Adam saw that Eve didn't die from eating the apple therefore convincing him that it must be ok to eat. This point in history is referred to as "the fall of man". It was Satan's first plot of deception, thus making Eve the first decoy in the history of the world.

> ....*So she took some of the fruit and ate it. Then she gave some to her husband, who was with her, and he ate it, too.*
> *Genesis 3:6*

Most any duck hunter will agree, duck calls are the icing on the cake when it comes to deception. As the modern duck call industry explodes into a multi-million dollar market, there's no other hunting item that receives more contemplation or requires more practice and technique. To those who have had the pleasure of witnessing it in action, there's nothing else in the world like seeing ducks make a decision mid-air in response to a call. Even ducks who exhibit a great deal of reservation about the quality of the camouflage and decoy spread can be lured in with the pleading whine of a well-articulated duck call.

The mallard hen call continues to be the most popular and most effective duck call in use since its inception in the mid-1800s. The popularity of the mallard hen call adds yet another point of correlation between ducks and humans, but should not come as much of a surprise to us (especially married) men. Regardless of our willingness to admit it or not; men and drake mallards alike tend to do as our significant other suggests. We all know the saying, "If Mama ain't happy, ain't nobody happy"! We, as men, may be the head of our households, but the woman in our life represents the neck muscles required to keep us "headed" in the right direction. It's highly unlikely that these roles will ever become reversed and a blind full of drake mallards trying to coerce a hen into a spread is as laughable as paying to see a marriage counselor that's on their 4th marriage. So, in conclusion, you could say that mallard drake calls may add some realistic qualities to your hunting situation by boosting the confidence of incoming ducks, but the true power of deception lies in the voice of the hen.

In addition to those ducks that may be buyin' in to what you're sellin', there's another group of ducks out there that some hunters refer to as "local ducks". These ducks represent the epitome of Christians in today's society. They've been around the block a time or two, have abounding knowledge about what's going on, know better than to give in to temptation, but still find it difficult to realize when they are being deceived. Ok, there was a lot in that last sentence.

- These ducks didn't just fly into town, they've been shot at more than once and they're skeptics.

- They've learned the routes to avoid, and usually hang out in the same areas day after day. Safety is their Goal.

So you may be asking now, what does this have to do with Christians? How many people do you know of that have been on a difficult road, but eventually saw the light and came to Christ after many years of flying in all the wrong places? Just like the ducks, they've probably lost friends and family members as a result of their poor choices, but they've learned from their mistakes. They may have found something that works for them and are now reluctant to deviate from the norm. Whether it's a special cornfield or place on the refuge for a duck, or the sanctuary of a nearby Church for humans, these ducks/people have found something that makes them feel invincible while they are there. In general, these people/ducks make extraordinary efforts to keep their nose down when traveling between their places of refuge because they are acutely aware of what may be lurking in the shadows.

- These ducks have abounding knowledge in the "real world" and have learned to keep their feathery butts on the straight and narrow.

> ....the gateway to life is very narrow and the road is
> difficult, and only a few ever find it.
> Matthew 7:14

Throughout the World, the moral standards of most cultures waiver very little from God's Ten Commandments, so it's relatively easy for most people to recognize right from wrong. Even if our "moral compass" is ignored, the effects of its alarm will likely continue to resonate throughout the heart of most men, ultimately resulting in some form of guilt. I've often struggled to understand if this is something we're born with, or if it's just instilled in us at such a young age that we feel like we were born with it. Regardless of when it is conceived, most of us have that sense of morality regardless of religion or spiritual background. It's not a result of becoming a Christian, but the choice to become a Christian brings about the awareness of right and wrong in one's actions. Remember, Adam and Eve ate from the tree of knowledge of good and evil giving them additional understanding about their condition.

> ....Then the eyes of both were opened, and
> they knew that they were naked.
> Genesis 3:7

Day after day, despite the vast amounts of knowledge we are able to acquire and the presence of a voice that tells us we know better, we continue to fly into hell's kitchen with wings cupped and landing gear extended. Even "local ducks" decide to work a decoy spread from time to time, but why do they choose to ignore the voice that tells them that they know better? The same reason Christians keep screwing it up on a daily basis, and will continue to do so until Jesus comes back.....Deception. Regardless of their well-planned and intentional flights down the narrow road to and from the Refuge, there's always a field in view that seems to have a better selection of food, maybe a more attractive mate, or a sweeter sounding call.

We are deceived on a regular basis; nicer shotguns, bigger trucks, faster boats, and even things that we would hold in high esteem as "good" things continue to get in the way. Maybe it's easy for most people to understand the correlation here with our society's "gotta have it" mentality, but it really gets grey when we discuss the reality of deception in seemingly "good" things. I won't beat around the bush here, we might as well start with something that most anyone (religious or not) would agree is a "good" thing. Church. Whether your definition refers only to a building, the activities inside the building, or just people that are gathered in the name of the Lord, the "Church" has some of the most nutrient rich soil for the roots of deception to take hold.

Ok, so before you go gettin' all upset thinking that I'm bashing your Church, give me a chance to explain. This is not my way of tearing apart the Church, this is only meant as a warning about the enemy's potential presence in the Church. Paul similarly justified his actions in his letter to the Church at Corinth:

….I do so with Christ's authority for your benefit, so that Satan will not outsmart us. For we are familiar with his evil schemes.
II Corinthians 2:11

Just as there are hunters sporting camouflage in every river bottom, rice field, or timber marsh across America every winter, churches across the nation are filled with camo-clad individuals on a weekly basis. No, it's not some new pattern that you're going to find at Bass Pro this winter, but "Church Camo" has become a popular attire for many Christians today. Today's society is well past the times of wearing your "Sunday Best" as a sign of reverence and respect. Most people's "everyday clothes" rival the quality of the common homesteader's "Sunday Best" worn when that tradition was practiced regularly. That being said, I do believe this tradition is still exercised to some degree, although in most cases, it's more of just a subconscious guideline rather than a common rule. In addition to our subconscious attempts to project a certain image among our peers with our Church clothes, there's more to "Church Camo" than just the clothes we wear. Not only do some Christians wear different clothes on Sunday than any other day of the week, many of them speak and act different as well. Christ didn't just call us to be his followers while we are at Church, he specified what we are supposed to do on a daily basis.

….If any of you wants to be my follower, you must turn from your selfish ways, take up your cross daily, and follow me.
Luke 9:23

Regardless of how or why we use "Church Camo", we must understand that we are all broken people. It's not a secret and God knows about it, so why must we put on a show for everyone else? Understanding the Gospel Message means that we wholeheartedly believe that no one is perfect or made righteous by their own doings, and we must accept that Jesus paid the ultimate price to give us freedom from our sin. If we truly understand this and believe it, why is there such an expectation for us to be holy that we must resort to impersonating perfect Christians?

> ....It is better to take refuge in the Lord than to trust in people.
> Psalm 118:8

Sure, there is an expectation put on every Christian in the world to be holy and righteous as Jesus was, but these expectations are inaccurately held by non-Christians. There is no reason to conceal your imperfectness among the presence of other Christians. Doing so is deceptive and only hinders our own development as Christians. We must be broken, humble, and honest amongst other believers in order to attain true Christian Fellowship. Again, I'm not singling out church-goers as your method of worship is not the point of contention here and I'm definitely not the model student. Rather, we all need to be aware of "Church Camo" and do our best not to use it in order to blend in with others around us who "seem" to have it all together. I hope you won't get too "offended" in the directness of my comments in this section, but my prayer would be for you to develop an understanding that these illustrations were used to show how deception can easily lead to corruption and how we need to be aware of its creeping presence within the Body of Christ, no matter how seemingly harmless it may present itself.

3 DISTRACTION

If you've ever driven down the "main drag" of most any populated city across the nation, you have probably been a victim of overwhelming distraction. Billboards, Neon Lights, Video Signs, Dancing Air Puppets, Spotlights...... they're all designed to do one thing.... get your attention! Of all the times that we should be alert and clearly focused on the task at hand, all of these things beg for the opportunity to break our concentration while we're DRIVING!. As we are all aware, a momentary lapse in attention or a split second delay in reaction can lead to fatal consequences on the road. So why do we allow these things to affect us? Human Nature I suppose, we're naturally drawn to use all of our available senses to take in as much information as possible at all times. Unfortunately, advertisers, merchandisers, and even Satan himself are well aware of this character flaw we all possess.

While the tactics of distraction may be subtle when applied to duck hunting, it doesn't make them any less effective. In some cases, our spiritual life included, the subtlety of a distraction can actually make it more effective as it can establish itself undetected for long periods of time. One highly effective, yet controversial piece of equipment used for duck hunting is the spinning wing decoy. Many states have outlawed the use of them as a result of a culture change in how ducks work a spread of decoys as well as reported changes in their specific feeding habits. Obviously, there's no regulatory service available for us humans that can watch out for our best interests without obstructing our God-given right of freewill, so we must manage these distractions based on our own knowledge and understanding.

Ultimately, distraction is not the threat that we are trying to identify and avoid. Distraction is usually just a tool in the act of deception. Spinning wing decoys are not what's driving the ducks to react differently, it's how they are used that causes the changes in behavior. These decoys are merely tools used in the overarching plan of deception for the hunting scenario. Distraction is really just a part of the plan. The spinning/flashing wing beats of these decoys draw the attention of unsuspecting ducks. This distraction leads the charge in the battle of deception followed by the presence of traditional decoys, the sound of duck calls, and the concealment of the actual threat.

Less obvious, but nearly as effective, some forms of distraction may be used as confidence boosters. For instance, motion decoys, pull strings, and quiver magnets are other highly useful tools for duck hunting, but these items will rarely grab a duck's attention from their standard aviation heights. These items are used to give your spread a realistic cherry on top so the ducks don't figure out your true intentions as quickly. Even reluctantly uncommitted ducks can be converted over by just a few ripples on the water making the entire spread seem more lifelike and authentic.

Christians are easily distracted too and subtlety seems to be the kryptonite used to infiltrate the lives of unsuspecting people. Just as deception can lie in seemingly good things, likewise can a distraction be a master of disguise. Many of the things we become distracted by are self-inflicted. Whether it's dual exhaust, fancy paint jobs, or ginormous spinning discs on the wheels of your car, everyone is franticly seeking individualism. I'm no exception, I enjoy my vehicles loud, high, and with big tires, but while I thoroughly enjoy these things when I look at my truck, the underlying truth is that these additions scream "look at me"! On the surface, we just want to be "different", but subconsciously, we're seeking approval from others. This may be a left field concept, but if you disagree with this idea, try not to smile or take any satisfaction in yourself the next time someone compliments your truck, boat, shotgun, or house. None of this is evil in itself, but too much effort in seeking our own individualism distracts us from the more important things in life.

Keeping with the theme of the more important things in life, Church is no exception to distractions. Remember, the focus is not supposed to be on doing Church, it's supposed to be about God and your relationship with Jesus Christ. Be careful not to get so caught up in programs, activities, or other Christian busy work that you overlook the reason you actually go to Church. I can tell you from experience, distractions in the Church are just as harmful as those outside the Church. When most all of the distractions contained within the Church are seemingly "good" things, it's extremely difficult to recognize when your focus on God is diminishing. I don't say these things to discourage you from getting involved in a Church, but want to issue a warning that your priority at Church should be worshipping our Creator and developing a relationship with his Son. Beyond these two things, we should be demonstrating to our kids how to build this relationship with Christ. They should see us engaged in true Christian

Fellowship, Prayer, and Bible Study as we develop knowledge and maturity during our walk with Christ. Serving within the Church is also important and necessary, but a careful balance should always be maintained so that the latter doesn't become a distraction and pull your focus away from God.

4 DUCK CALLS, REALLY?

Duck Calls?.....what can we possibly learn from a duck call?

First off, in order to answer this question, I believe we have to begin with a different question: Is it possible to share your Faith in Christ using objects or situations that have no relevance to Religion, Spirituality, or even Christ himself? Jesus did it with astounding success, and I don't believe for a second that he did it this way because he was just showing off. He set the example. He used parables that were simple, easy to understand, and had practical meaning for his audience. His parables related everyday life to deeper Spiritual Themes so believers could better comprehend the complexity of his teachings even in the presence of prideful and hesitant non-believers. Even in today's society, we should be able to use common objects or situations from everyday life to convey God's message to an audience that may be unwilling to listen or pay attention in a traditional setting.

Now don't misconstrue what I'm suggesting here. This is not an attempt to sell a car, so I'm not offering a loophole to use the old "bait and switch" model. It's not about deception or witnessing to someone via subliminal messages without them knowing what you're up to. This is about meeting a person in their comfort zone and using common interests you may have with a person to establish a connection with them. Relationships are built on trust, so know that your true intentions will be obvious. I've seen evangelistic efforts fail on more than one occasion because of their true intentions. While most any evangelistic effort in the name of Christ is likely conceived as a well-meaning tool for "spreading the word", much of "The Great Commission" gets lost as the effort is put into motion.

> ....Therefore, go and make disciples of all the nations, baptizing them in the name of the Father and the Son and the Holy Spirit.
> Matthew 28:19

Priorities are set and the focus becomes: How many people can we reach? I call this "Splash & Dash Evangelism". You establish an opportunity to chat with someone, they verbalize the "Sinner's Prayer", you invite them to Church to be Baptized, and then dash on to the next person you can find that will listen. Doing it this way has now instituted a "Production Goal" on a personal directive from Jesus Christ. At this point, it's no longer about the purpose, it's merely a "pissing contest" that uses the number of people "reached" to measure how "Christian" we are. Discipleship is a major component that gets lost using "Splash & Dash Evangelism". Not only is Discipleship a key component in the "The Great Commission", it's the FIRST thing mentioned! Making disciples takes effort, and there's more to it than reading a few lines off of a card and having someone repeat a prayer. Discipleship goes back to my previous comments about establishing a relationship with someone. This relationship has to be authentic in nature and there's no better way to make that type of connection with someone than to find something you have in common with them.

Back to the duck call question. I believe it's absolutely possible to make spiritual connections with people over objects, situations, or experiences that have no religious affiliation whatsoever. Just as Jesus used parables about everyday life, we should be able to talk about what we know or have in common and relate that to our Faith in Christ so that others are invited to understand with no strings attached. Taking that thought process a step further, God has given me intimate knowledge, skills, and abilities pertaining to duck calls. How do you glorify God with a duck call? I've asked myself this question many times over the course of several years and the answer always develops itself a little more each time I ask. I challenge you to ask this question for yourself: What can I do to glorify God? As we continue through the next chapters, I'd ask that you think about this on your own terms. What is it that you have in common with other people that you could use to show the Glory of God to someone in a non-traditional setting?

5 DUCK CALLS, GLORIFYING GOD?

So, how exactly do you go about glorifying God with a duck call? I can't tell you about the numerous conversations I've had with myself about this (some of which became heated and resulted in name-calling...), but I can lead you through the steps that have gotten me to the point I'm at now. Keep in mind, as you've probably figured out already, I'm no professional writer...don't claim to be, and don't want to become one! It's rather ironic for me to be writing a book anyway, because I can count the number of books I've read since High School on one hand. I'm just not much on reading, I'd rather wait for the movie! At times throughout this venture, I've honestly felt similar to the way Moses felt when God was revealing his plan to him.

> *But Moses pleaded with the Lord, "O Lord, I'm not very good with words. I never have been, and I'm not now, even though you have spoken to me. I get tongue-tied and my words get tangled."*
> *Exodus 4:10*

That being said, I hope this in some way makes sense to you and will lead you to what God has in store for your life. How do you glorify God with _____?

How do you glorify God with _____? *(you fill in the blank)*

✓ Pray Wholeheartedly

God wants to know that you are truly at his disposal. When you pray....mean it! Half-hearted prayers will likely yield half-hearted results.

> *"If you look for me wholeheartedly, you will find me."*
> Jermiah29:13

✓ Listen for God's direction

Whether it's reading the Bible, listening to Christian music, or just sitting in silence, let God speak to you. In today's world, there's little chance for God to get a word in edgewise.

> *"....and they follow him, for they recognize his voice."*
> John 10:4

✓ Inquire about your options

Everything's not always black and white. Talk around and be creative, your Godly purpose is not likely to be the same as anyone else's, so don't expect to replicate anyone else's journey.

> *"...seek, and you will find..."* Matthew 7:7

✓ Do Something

Don't make excuses. Putting it off isn't going to help anyone. Decide what you want to do, and go do it. Waiting until you're more mature, more comfortable, or more knowledgeable are all excuses. If you took the first two steps seriously, God will be there to guide you through whatever you decide to do.

> *"...do it with enthusiasm, as to the Lord and not to people."*
> Colossians 3:23

I wish I could tell you that the journey to this point for me was as straightforward as it may seem from the four bullet points previously mentioned, but those simple notes have come from several years of trial and error which just so happens to be the way that I learn the best. I've looked for many ways to glorify God with a duck call. From donating the proceeds of every tenth call I sold on eBay, to tithing exactly 10% on every call I sold, I tried several things to justify my infatuation with duck calls as a Godly venture. Unfortunately, none of these were overly fulfilling and I always heard a voice in the back of my head saying, "Is that it?". So I claimed to pray about it, not really knowing what I was praying for, but going through the motions to see what would happen. What happened was nothing until I asked the question to a friend of mine over the phone who could tell I was agonizing over it. Shortly after asking him, "How do I glorify God with a duck call?", we were knee-deep in creative ideas for a new duck call which I didn't even realize was the answer to my question.

Over the next two years, I worked on the duck call off and on with an unannounced calling on my life that this needed to be done, but I was still oblivious to its purpose. Ok, to address your question, two years seems rather ridiculous for a duck call, but for now, let's just say the design was rather intricate and complicated. Details were overwhelming at times to the point that I needed to put it away and work on something else. After starting on this duck call that was conceived over the phone after a seemingly silly question, my family's spiritual life flourished and we grew closer to God than we'd ever been before despite my wife and I both being "saved" as a child. We realized that our commitment to the Lord as an adult was totally different than the choice we made as a child. Neither of us following our decision with Baptism as children, we were Baptized together as an outward expression of a change in our heart and lives as a result of our commitment to God as adults. We also developed many meaningful relationships with other believers that eventually led to the conception of a CD and music ministry with a few close friends. Not knowing where any of this was going, I continued working on playing guitar, writing songs, and developing a concept that we'd not really seen before.

One afternoon, as I returned home from dropping my Mom off at the airport, it came a gully washer as I was driving down the interstate forcing me to turn off the radio and concentrate on just keeping the truck from hydroplaning off the highway. As the weather broke and the sun came through the clouds, I continued home with the radio off as I felt God starting to reveal things to me. By the time I made it home, he had me convinced that we needed a recording studio in order to record the CD's for the Ministry. Having a bit of unused space in our basement and myself with decent construction skills, I knew what needed to happen. Now, this wasn't justification for me to have a recording studio in the house. I'm nowhere near a decent enough musician or singer to even consider that this was a dream of mine or anything. I had absolutely no use for a recording studio, but this Ministry idea we'd had was going to need somewhere to record audio that was quiet and also provided an area where all of the equipment could be setup and left unattended without fear that the kids would decide to start singing karaoke and potentially turn the microphone cables into lassos!

After I was charged with the task, the next obstacle was to figure out how to pay for it which turned me back to the duck call that's been two years in the making. After a conversation or two of explaining what God had put on my heart, my friend who'd helped me develop the design on this duck call asked me what I wanted for it. I hadn't put much thought into it since it wasn't even finished, but I gave him a price of $800 anyway. I didn't hear a word from him for nearly two days. I was afraid I may have given him sticker shock, but the next e-mail from him was a simple one-liner saying "Check your Paypal account". Confused and strangely excited, I found $1,000 in my account and a message that followed saying "Just get it done when you can".

God really does work in mysterious ways, and this was definitely not what I had in mind for the funds I'd be making off this duck call. I'd already reverted back to my self-satisfying wants and desires thinking I'd probably get a new set of wheels for my truck when I sold that call. Little did I know, God had a plan for it all along. So, without drawing it out any longer, the funds were used to build the studio, buy the equipment, and get the Ministry started as we'd planned. The duck call was finished shortly after and went on to win 1st Place in the Amateur Carving Division at the Callmaker & Collectors Association of America's Fancy Call Contest in 2012. The call features a scene from the story of Noah's Ark, but it's depicted with sporting animals. It includes 2 Elk, 2 Whitetail Deer, 2 Turkeys, 2 Ducks, and 2 Geese. One side of the insert shows a dove being released out of the ark while the other side shows the dove returning with an olive branch in its mouth.

The Noah's Ark Duck Call

6 DUCK CALLS, WHERE TO START?

For starters, before we can get into the makings of a duck call, we need to grow a tree. I refer to the next illustration as the "Christianity Tree". This may remind you of something similar to the "Circle of Life", but this concept continues to spread, gaining momentum, and ends with eternity rather than decomposing remains.

The Christianity Tree

- *"The seed is planted..."*

Someone told you about Christ. Old or young, in America these days, most everyone has been exposed to the Gospel at some point or another in their lives.

- **"The watering of the seed..."**

  You're convicted by the Holy Spirit about what you've been told, what you've read, or your own interpretation of the meaning of life as you read the Bible.

- **"The seed sprouts..."**

  You accept Christ as your savior. You make this decision based on the internal convictions of your heart, but act on the choice through your own freewill.

- **"The tree develops roots and matures..."**

  You begin your walk with Christ. You continue to grow in character and knowledge through prayer, Bible study, and commitment.

- **"The tree bears fruit and new seeds are planted..."**

  You share your Faith in Christ with others. Whether it's through direct testimony, leading by example, or using whatever Spiritual Gift the Lord has blessed you with, you express your Faith in all you do to everyone around you.

Witnessing to others may seem impossible at times and is usually something that makes most anyone a bit apprehensive or reserved, but it really should be as simple as living in the context of the Christianity Tree. We don't always have to set out with a specific goal of witnessing to others for it to actually happen. Everyday life happens all the time, and it's one of the best ways to meet people in their own situation and show them the love of Christ. Don't limit your witnessing/sharing of your Faith to one day a week or only during specific Church-Sponsored initiatives.

> *"You are the light of the world ...... No one lights a lamp*
> *and then puts it under a basket. Instead, a lamp is placed*
> *on a stand, where it gives light to everyone in the house.*
> *Matthew 5:14-15*

Continuing on with the tree illustration, we can also correlate the needs of a tree with the needs of Christians:

Needs of the Tree

Sun = God
Water = Bible
Nutrients = Christian Fellowship

Just as there are many different species of trees, there are also many varieties of Christians. The needs outlined above are somewhat vague, but fully cover the necessities needed for either to survive. There are more specific things to look at here as well though; what does it take for either subject to thrive? Some trees require a specific climate, amount of water, or particular nutrient in the soil to really thrive and become the best version of their species that they can become. Christians are no different and this may help explain why there's so many diverse variations of Worship Services, Sunday School Classes, and Missions Opportunities. Everyone has certain needs in order to thrive, but it should not always be the burden of the Church to accommodate every kind of "tree". Some "trees" may not survive in certain climates because of their specific needs, but this doesn't mean that there aren't other "trees" that can and will thrive in that environment. Sometimes, there may be a need to support transplantation rather than to continue nursing a few "trees" on life support.

The needs of the tree are not the only thing that can be correlated to the Christian life.   Dangers to the tree can also be used to represent struggles in the life of Christians:

Just like a tree, prolonged exposure to "SIN" can have serious effects on a Christian. If you remember the analogy between water and the Bible, a drought, or severe lack of "scripture" can also cause a Christian to wither.

7 DUCK CALLS, THE PROCESS

So the likely question you have now is, how's he going to turn cutting the tree down into some type of Religious experience?? Nope, I don't have a great correlation here to continue the illustration, but it does remind me of an interesting cartoon about sacrifice.

We are called to sacrifice ourselves to the service of the Lord. Obviously, not in a mortal sense, but in that we should put aside our selfish desires and make God a priority in our lives.

> "...offer your bodies as living sacrifices that are holy and pleasing to God, for this is the reasonable way to worship."
> Romans 12:1

Moving forward, we'll be shifting gears from the Christian being like a tree, to the creation of a duck call being similar to the way God forms us into what he has envisioned for our lives.

Useful Pieces

A truckload of freshly cut timber is not what you would order to get started making duck calls. The trees have to first be processed into manageable pieces. God puts us through a similar process before we can become useful for his purpose. Through trials, conviction, and knowledgeable counsel, God can whittle away unnecessary, inessential, inappropriate, and irrelevant things in our lives. In addition to milling the lumber into smaller pieces, it also has to go through a grading process that sorts each piece of wood into categories according to each piece's distinguishing characteristics. Just as every part of the tree may not be suitable for making duck calls, every Christian is not called to be a Pastor, Evangelist, or even Sunday School Teacher.

> *"For the body itself is not made up of only one part, but of many parts." I Corinthians 12:14*

The God-Shaped Hole

Once the lumber has been milled into useful pieces, the first step in the creation of a duck call is drilling the hole.

Every human being on Earth is created with a God-Shaped hole in their spirit that longs to be filled. Many will attempt to fill this void within themselves using their choice of what they feel they "need". For some it may be alcohol, drugs, or just food, but for others it can become extreme determination in their job, seeking approval from others, or an infatuation with filling their lives with "stuff". The truth of the matter is, there's only one thing that will fill this void successfully and deliver the peace and satisfaction that everyone is so frantically searching for.

Tools of the Trade

Moving on with the process of making a duck call, after boring a hole in a piece of wood, it's probably obvious that you'll need a special tool of some sort that allows you to mount the blank onto the lathe. The essential piece of equipment that makes this possible is called a mandrel.

In definition, a mandrel is a tool that grabs hold of a workpiece to keep it from spinning out of control while it's being shaped or formed. Conceptually, this isn't much different than the method Christ uses to mold and shape us into the person he wants us to be.

> *"It's not that I have already reached this goal or have already been perfected, but I pursue it, so that I may achieve it because Christ grabbed hold of me for just this purpose.*
> *Philippians 3:12*

Rough Around the Edges

Once the blank is mounted on the lathe, the blank must be "roughed out". This primarily consists of turning the lathe on and knocking off the square corners of the blank, but in technical terms, it's a preliminary cutting or carving process that removes the bulk of any unwanted material. As the tool is worked back and forth across the length of the workpiece, the blank becomes smoother with each pass.

As you've probably already guessed this comparison, God does the same with us once he grabs hold of our lives and begins the shaping process.

> *"Close the book on evil, God, but publish your mandate for us. You get us ready for life: you search for our soft spots, you knock off our rough edges."*
> *Psalm 7:9*

The Trinity at Work

As I mentioned earlier, God has a way of grabbing hold of us from the inside. This task is performed by the Holy Spirit which is the part of the Trinity that lives inside of us and gives us moral guidance, inner peace, and helps facilitate Godly understanding. Envision the diagram below as a view of a duck call blank from the end with the hole in it.

Just as a mandrel holds the duck call blank from the inside, the Holy Spirit lives inside of us as a piece of God himself. This "new heart" that we've been given longs to please God and give up our sinful desires. We have to submit ourselves to his control and let him start to lead us not only on Sundays, but in every aspect of our lives.

As God fills us from within our own heart, we start to recognize his power and understand that we are his creation. So, as the lathe is turned on during the process of making a duck call, so does God use his power to spin our lives in order to shape us into his creation.

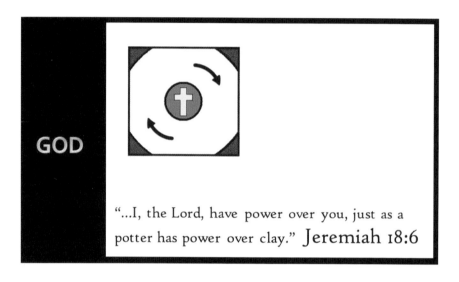

GOD

"...I, the Lord, have power over you, just as a potter has power over clay." Jeremiah 18:6

As the shaping begins, an additional tool must be introduced to start removing the rough edges. This tool must be strong, sturdy, and sharp.

Just as the duck call blank is turned to remove the rough edges; once we accept Jesus as our Savior, he immediately starts working to remove the rough edges in our lives that hold us back from fulfilling our purpose as a follower of his.

selfishness   bitterness

deceit

PRIDE   laziness

jealousy

GREED

JESUS   "Jesus Christ himself is the foundation. No one can make another one."   1 Corinthians 3:11

With each cut of the tool, we become closer to the creation he has in mind for us to be.

8 DUCK CALLS,
THE GREAT COMMISION

"Go therefore and make disciples of all nations, baptizing them in the name of the Father, the Son, and the Holy Spirit, teaching them to observe all that I have commanded you..."
Matthew 28:19-20

There are millions of people in the world, each with their own specific attributes, physical characteristics, and specialties. Even with the unfathomable number of different types of people, we are all called to one task after accepting Christ as our personal Savior. Duck calls are similar in that the vessels carrying out the task are all different and many with specific purposes. Coming in all shapes, sizes, and colors, some are well-dressed with carvings or decoration that are pleasing to the eye. Others are well articulated and crafted to carry premium tonal qualities. Some can have sharp edges, many are made with unique materials, and even those made from the same materials will always have a uniqueness specific to itself.

The message is always the same, but it requires multiple delivery methods to become effective for a given audience. Whether it's a soft timber call, a loud open water call, or a decorative collector call that sits on a shelf, they all have the responsibility of fulfilling their purpose in life as a duck call. So, what makes it a duck call? If you'll notice in the previous picture, only one part of the call is shown. This picture only shows the barrel of several duck calls. The barrel is not what makes it a duck call, just like a person is not what makes them a Christian. The barrel is just the microphone needed to help facilitate the projection of what is being said. Simply put, it's what's inside that counts. Next we'll cover the parts that go inside of a duck call to make it sound like a duck. There are two different types of duck calls shown below, but the parts are similar in both designs.

Regardless of which type of duck call we are discussing, they both use a three part system to create the proper sound needed to be used effectively. This three part system can also be used to help describe the Holy Trinity recognized within the Christian Faith.

The toneboard is the backbone of the call and will ultimately determine what type of sound the call will produce. The shape, stability, and finish of the toneboard must be perfect.

> *"As for God, his way is perfect: The Lord's word is flawless..."*
> *2 Samuel 22:31*

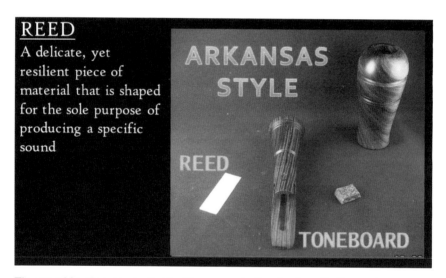

The reed is also essential to the sound of a duck call. It can be shaped or trimmed to target a specific type of call, but it's only purpose is to produce the sound of the call.

"It was a perfect sacrifice by a perfect person
to perfect some very imperfect people."
Hebrews 10:14

The material the reed is made of must also be capable of handling extreme torture, bending and sacrificing itself to different variations in order to maintain the integrity of the call regardless of the amount of pressure introduced to the call.

The wedge, regardless of the style of call or material used, is the final piece that locks the Trinity together. It gives support to the reed and is the integral part of the duck call that makes the barrel of the call useful in fulfilling its overall purpose.

"In the same way, the Spirit also joins to help in our weakness..."
Romans 8:26

In closing, you can now see that there are three things that must work together to produce the proper sound of a duck call. In order for the call to project its message, the three parts of the Trinity must be present and functioning. The loss or lack of any part will cause the duck call to become inoperable. Essentially, in both the duck call world as well as the life of a Christian, it's what's on the inside that counts.

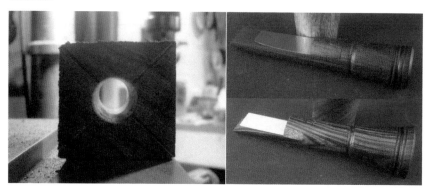

As these three things come together to fill the God-Shaped hole, it's possible for Christians and duck hunters alike to project their message from the highest mountain tops to the lowest hunting pits of the World.

> *"And there are three who give testimony in heaven, the Father, the Son, and the Holy Spirit. And these three are one."*
> *I John 5:7*

ABOUT THE AUTHOR

Benjamin "Bear" Lyle is a self-taught custom callmaker that's been in the business since 2004. Specializing in Arkansas and Reelfoot Style duck calls, he offers calls made from several different types of wood. Custom options are also available that include carving, laminating, and hand-painting just to name a few. Benjamin has also won multiple awards from National organizations such as the NWTF and Callmaker & Collectors Association of America for both his Decorative and Hunting Class duck calls.

With a family of five and a full-time career, callmaking is just a hobby, but still a very effective way to make duck season last throughout the entire year! Benjamin resides in Clarksville, TN with his wife Jessica and their three girls Breanna, Jordan, and Kalyn.

More information can be found @
www.BEARKRAFT.com

or

Like us on Facebook @ **BearKraft Game Calls**

or

Follow us on Twitter at **@BearKraft**

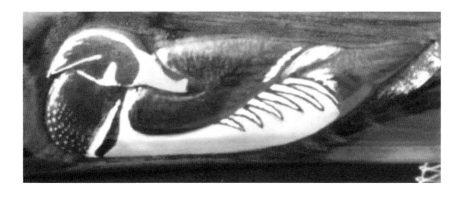

49209432R10028

Made in the USA
Lexington, KY
29 January 2016